CW00665071

ꝫ

—

the world premiere of

Katherine Desouza

by Nick Stafford

First performed on 6 May 2006
at The Door,
Birmingham Repertory Theatre

Birmingham Repertory Theatre
Centenary Square
Broad Street
Birmingham
B1 2EP

www.birmingham-rep.co.uk.

Katherine Desouza

by Nick Stafford

Kevin Cross Russell Layton

Fay White Emma Pallant

David Desouza Paul McCleary

Emile Ged McKenna

Director Gwenda Hughes

Designer Matthew Wright

Lighting Designer Simon Bond

Composer and Sound Designer
Jon Nicholls

Stage Manager Darren Abel

Deputy Stage Manager
Emma Ledsam

**Assistant Stage Manager
Apprentice** Hannan Finnegan

Cast and Company

Kevin
Russell Layton

Russell trained at the Webber Douglas Academy.

Theatre credits include: *Blue Remembered Hills* (New Vic Theatre, Stoke); *A Chaste Maid In Cheapside* (Almeida Theatre); *Henry IV (i and ii), Henry V, Romeo And Juliet, The Comedy Of Errors* (Royal Shakespeare Company); *Salome* (International tour); *The Crucible, Coriolanus* (West Yorkshire Playhouse); *Coriolanus* (Mermaid Theatre); *You See The Thing Is This* (The Gate Theatre); *Hanuman* (National Theatre); *Ruffian On The Stair* (Haymarket Theatre, Leicester); *Peter Pan* (Theatr Clwyd); *Dr. Faustus* (Nuffield Theatre, Southampton); *Of Mice And Men* (Southwark Playhouse); *Bedroom Farce* (English Theatre Frankfurt); *The Jewess Of Toledo* (Bridewell); *A Midsummer Night's Dream* (Cannizaro Park); *Rat In The Skull* (Grove Theatre)

Television credits include: *EastEnders, Great Inventions, Holby City, Clitheroe, The Bill, The Upper Hand, These Colours Don't Run, Fist Of The Dragonfly, Nightclub*

Film credits include: *Transvision, Diary Of An Actor*

David
Paul McCleary

Theatre credits include: *Hysteria* (Exeter); *Richard II* (Ludlow Festival); *Othello* (USA tour); *To Kill A Mockingbird, Beauty And The Beast, Once A Catholic, Billy Liar, The Tempest, Hamlet, The Railway Children, Dead Funny, Othello, Waiting For Godot, David Copperfield, The Cherry Orchard, An Inspector Calls,* (New Vic Theatre, Stoke); *Krapp's Last Tape* (Derby Dance Centre); *Much Ado About Nothing, All's Well That Ends Well, Romeo And Juliet* (Actors London Stage); *Insignificance, The Weir, Waiting For Godot* (Northampton Theatre Royal); *Broken Glass* (Watford/Salisbury); *The Tempest, Much Ado About Nothing, The Merchant Of Venice, The Danton Affair, The Taming Of The Shrew* (Royal Shakespeare Company); *Hove, On, Juno And The Paycock,* (Royal National Theatre); *Hamlet* (Oxford Stage Company); *The Woman In White* (Greenwich); *Hamlet* (Young Vic); *Operation Elvis* (Almeida Theatre); *Difficult Times* (Riverside Studios); *Funny Peculiar; Cinderella* (Derby Playhouse); *Pinnochio* (Manchester Library Theatre); *Edward II, Class Enemy* (Bristol Old Vic); *See You Next Tuesday, On My Own Two Feet, Hamlet* (Sheffield Crucible); *Henry IV Part One, Moll Flanders* (Croydon Warehouse); *You're A Good Man Charlie Brown, Tom Foolery, A View From The Bridge, Privates On Parade, Salonika, While The Sun Shines, Mr. Bolfry, Bent* (Edinburgh Lyceum); *A Night In Peking/The Story Of Aladdin, Snapshots, Hamlet, All Our Loving, Theatre Royal Follies,*

The Football Apprentices, Sisters, The Hottest Bet In Town (Theatre Royal Stratford East); The Golden Pathway Annual, The Adventures Of A Bear Called Paddington, A Man For All Seasons (Liverpool Playhouse); Loot, Measure For Measure (Contact Theatre, Manchester)

Television credits include: Outlaws, Max And Paddy, The Bill, All Good Things, Boon, Billy Play For Today, No Pasaran, Peak Practice

Film credits include: Calendar Girls, Prostitute, Brittania Hospital

Emile
Ged McKenna

Theatre credits include: The Lonesome West (Hull Truck Theatre); Kes, Cleo, Camping, Emmanuelle And Dick, Toad Of Toad Hall, Big Maggie, 2nd From Last In The Sack Race, Translations (New Vic Theatre, Stoke); Iron (Royal Court Theatre); The Rise And Fall Of Little Voice (Oldham Coliseum); Iron (Traverse Theatre; The Rise And Fall Of Little Voice (Bury St. Edmunds); Things We Do For Love (Salisbury Playhouse); Wuthering Heights (West Yorkshire Playhouse); Yard (The Bush); Mother Courage And Her Children, Waiting For Godot (Contact Theatre); The Farmer's Bride by Ged McKenna (Stephen Joseph Theatre, Scarborough/BAC, London and tour); The Tempest, Desire Under The Elms (Shared Experience); The Oginsky Polonaise (The Gate Theatre); Romeo And Juliet (Cannizaro Park); A House By The Sea (BAC); Macbeth (Cheek By Jowl);

Woyzek (Astra Theatre Company); The Shaugraun, Bartholemew Fair, Ghetto (Royal National Theatre)

Television credits include: Fantabuloso, Casualty, The Bill, No Angels, Merseybeat, Murphy's Law, A Wing And A Prayer, Brookside, The Locksmith, Boon, The Paradise Club, The Long Roads

Film credits include: Vanity Fair, Shirley Valentine

Radio credits include: Rhythm On The Ceiling

Fay
Emma Pallant

Theatre credits include: Cymbeline (Regents Park Theatre); Pedro The Great Pretender, House Of Desires, Dog In A Manger, Tamar's Revenge, As You Like It, Henry IV Parts I and II, Laughter In The Dark (Royal Shakespeare Company); Project B (Tristan Bates Theatre); Precious Bane (Pentabus, UK Tour); She Stoops To Conquer, A Laughing Matter (Lyttleton Theatre and UK Tour); Romeo And Juliet (New Vic Theatre, Stoke and Creation Theatre, Oxford); Prometheus In Evin (Brockley Jack Theatre); The Tempest (Landor Theatre); A Week With Tony (Steam Industry, Finborough); The Orchard Skins (Lakeside Theatre); Sideways Moving (Edinburgh Festival)

Television and film credits include: Hello You!; Wake Up; Macbeth; The Biker's Opera

Radio credits include: Daughter Of The Air

Nick Stafford
Writer

Stage plays include: *The Canal Ghost, The Whisper Of Angels' Wings* (Birmingham Repertory Theatre); *Moll Cutpurse* (Avon Touring); *The Snow Queen* (Library Theatre and New Vic); *Listen With dA dA*, (Serpentine Gallery); *The Devil's Only Sleeping* (Coventry Belgrade and Birmingham Repertory Theatre); *The Go Between* (Northampton Theatre Royal); *Battle Royal* (National Theatre); *Luminosity* (Royal Shakespeare Company); *Love Me Tonight* (Hampstead Theatre)

Radio plays include: *A Matter Of Sex* (winner Sony Gold Award Best Original Script); *Ring of Roses, La Petite Mort, The List, A Year And A Day, The Fire Inside, Birdsong, A Thousand Acres, Frankenstein*

TV films include; *The Missing Finger*

Screenplays include: *The Blue Suit* and *Pity* (Winner of Dennis Potter Play Of The Year Award 1998)

Nick was writer in residence at Birmingham Repertory Theatre from 1997 to 1998. His current work in progress includes *War Horse* to be staged at the Royal National Theatre in 2007, and his first novel *Armistice.*

Gwenda Hughes
Director

Gwenda graduated from Liverpool University and then worked as an actor in theatres in Manchester, Liverpool, Plymouth, Watford and Leicester; and in TV with the BBC and Granada. In 1982 she was awarded the Arts Council Trainee Directors Bursary to work with Theatre Centre Young Peoples Theatre,

commissioning and directing new work for young people.

A year later she was appointed Artistic Director of Watford Palace Theatre In Education Company, where she introduced work with and for young people with severe learning disabilities.

Gwenda became the Associate Director of Birmingham Repertory Theatre in 1990, and directed over twenty productions including *All My Sons, Hobson's Choice, Romeo And Juliet, Nothing Compares To You, Whispers Of Angels Wings* and *Once On This Island* which transferred to the West End and won an Olivier Award for Best Musical.

Since 1998 Gwenda has been Artistic Director and Chief Executive of the New Vic Theatre, North Staffordshire, where her productions include *Smoke, Once We Were Mothers, A Woman Of No Importance, Kes, Romeo And Juliet, By Jeeves, Who's Afraid Of Virginia Woolf, Moll Flanders, The Wizard Of Oz, Office Suite, Broken Glass, A Passionate Woman, The Tenant Of Wildfell Hall* and *Othello.*

Matthew Wright
Designer

Matthew trained at the Glasgow School of Art in Textile Design.

Designs for theatre include *Speaking Like Magpies* (Royal Shakespeare Company); *One Under* (Tricycle); *Clouds* (UK tour); *Paper Thin* (Kali Theatre); *Us And Them, The Dead Eye Boy* (Hampstead); *The Green Man, Presence, Royal Supreme, Blood Red Saffron Yellow, Musik, The Imposter* (Theatre Royal Plymouth); *Summer Lightning, Amy's View* (Salisbury), *Arcadia* (Theatre Royal Northampton);

Dancing At Lughnasa, Four Nights In Knaresborough, All That Trouble We Had (New Victoria Theatre, Stoke); *Private Lives, Charley's Aunt* (Northcott Exeter); *Larkin With Women* (West Yorkshire Playhouse); *The Deep Blue Sea, Neville's Island, A Taste Of Honey* (Watford Palace); *Confusions, Habeus Corpus* (Salisbury); *Summer Lightning* (Salisbury & Theatre Royal Bath); *The End Of The Affair* (Salisbury/Bridewell); *Our Country's Good* (Edinburgh Lyceum); *Hamlet* (NT Education); *Woman In Mind* (Theatre Royal York); *Twelfth Night, Hamlet* (OSC); *Romeo And Juliet* (Greenwich) and *Pow!* (Paines Plough). Other designs for Birmingham Repertory Theatre include *Bezhti, Getting To The Foot Of The Mountain, Swamp City, Bells* and *Chaos* (Kali Theatre Company), and *On The Ceiling,* which also played in the West End.

Opera credits include *Ii Pomo D'oro* (Batignano Opera Festival) and *Don Pasquale* (Scottish Opera Go Round).

Matthew also designed the costumes for *Seriously Funny* for Channel Four Television.

Simon Bond
Lighting Designer

Simon works as a lighting technician at The REP and has been designing an increasing number of shows for The Door. Most recently these have included *Bolt Hole, The Santaland Diaries* and *Seasons Greetings To All Our Friends And Family,* and the Young REP's production of *Kill Jill.* He recently worked with Pentabus Theatre for their touring production of Alecky Blythe's *Strawberry Fields,* and his favourite colour is pink.

Jon Nicholls
Composer and Sound Designer

Jon Nicholls studied composition at the London College Of Music, and electroacoustic music at Dartington.

Theatre work includes: *Amadeus* and *Masterclass* (Derby Playhouse); *Silas Marner, Art, Blue Remembered Hills* and *The Changeling* (Theatr Clwyd); *The Seamstress' Revenge* (Birmingham Repertory Theatre); *Danny King Of The Basement* (Sheffield Crucible); *The Rivals, Alice In Wonderland* and *Therese Raquin* (Basingstoke Haymarket); *Hansel And Gretal, Hamlet, Nosferatu, Nicholas Nickleby, The Love-Child, The Legend Of King Arthur* and *Get Carter* (Red Shift)

Screen work includes: *Spiked, Sex On The Streets, Undercover Teacher, Nuclear Ginza, Women Facing War* and *Small Pain For Glory.*

Film work includes: *Shore, Lena, Every Little Thing, Karain, The Hurlers, Kushe, My Constant Companion* and *The Havamal.*

Jon has also recently composed music for *Between Friends* for BBC Radio 4, and is currently developing an opera, *Falling Across,* due to be staged as part of this year's Collide Festival in Birmingham. He is also a regular performer, composer and teacher of Javanese gamelan.

Birmingham Repertory Theatre Company

$_{THE}$ REP

$_{THE}$REP

Birmingham Repertory Theatre

Birmingham Repertory Theatre is one of Britain's leading national producing theatre companies. Under the recent Artistic Direction of Jonathan Church, The REP has enjoyed great success with a busy and exciting programme, and we are now proud to announce Rachel Kavanaugh as the new Artistic Director. We look forward to announcing her first season of work later this year.

The REP's productions regularly transfer to London, tour nationally and internationally. Recent transfers and tours have included *Glorious!, The Birthday Party, The Witches, Through The Woods, Of Mice And Men, A Doll's House, The Crucible, Celestina, Hamlet, The Ugly Eagle, The Old Masters, The Snowman, The Gift, Behsharam* (*Shameless*) and *The Ramayana*.

The commissioning and production of new work lies at the core of The REP's programme. The Door was established eight years ago as a theatre dedicated to the production and presentation of new writing. In this time, it has given world premieres to new plays from a new generation of British playwrights including Abi Morgan, Moira Buffini, Bryony Lavery, Crispin Whittell, Paul Lucas, Gurpreet Kaur Bhatti, Sarah Woods, Roy Williams, Kaite O'Reilly, Ray Grewal, Jess Walters, Jonathan Harvey, Tamsin Oglesby, Sarah Daniels, Shan Khan, Arzhang Pezhman and Nick Stafford. The REP itself received The Peggy Ramsey Award for New Writing, enabling us to develop and commission more new plays for the future.

The Door aims to provide a distinct alternative to the work seen in the Main House: a space where new voices and contemporary stories can be heard, and to create new audiences for the work of the company. The Door is also a place to explore new ideas and different approaches to making theatre, to develop new plays and support emerging companies. It also emphasises work for and by young people, through *Transmissions*, our *First Stages* children's theatre programme and the strong emphasis on work with living writers in *Young REP*, our youth theatre initiative.

Transmissions – our young writers' programme – gives writers aged 12 to 25 the opportunity to work with professional playwrights to develop initial ideas into complete scripts. In July the writers come

REP
Birmingham Repertory Theatre

---

together with professional actors and directors to present a showcase of their work in the *Transmissions Festival*. *Transmissions* also has an outreach programme supported by the Paul Hamlyn Foundation, with schools from across the region participating.

'Transmissions hurtled into its second week, blazing with energy and delivering some of the most provocative and original new work to be seen anywhere in the city'   Birmingham Post

'A rich and extraordinary assortment of tomorrow's talent'
                                                   Evening Mail

'It is a brilliant enterprise'   Birmingham Post

For more information about the work of The Door or about our work with new writers, please contact Ben Payne or Caroline Jester on 0121 245 2000. If you are a young writer and want more information about how to apply for *Transmissions*, please send your contact details to Ben Musgrave at ben.musgrave@birmingham-rep.co.uk (or call on 0121 245 2045), and we will contact you when we advertise for submissions.

Artistic Director **Rachel Kavanaugh**
Executive Director **Stuart Rogers**
Associate Director (Literary) **Ben Payne**

Book online at www.birmingham-rep.co.uk

Birmingham Repertory Theatre is a registered charity, number 223660

Nick Stafford
Katherine Desouza

ff

faber and faber

First published in 2006
by Faber and Faber Limited
3 Queen Square London WC1N 3AU

Typeset by Country Setting, Kingsdown, Kent CT14 8ES
Printed in England by Mackays of Chatham plc, Chatham, Kent

A CIP record for this book
is available from the British Library

ISBN 0–571–23376–7
ISBN 978–0–571–23376–2

2 4 6 8 10 9 7 5 3 1

For Ben Payne

without whom this play –
like many others – wouldn't exist

Characters

David

Kevin

Fay

Emile

*The actor playing Emile also doubles
as the non-speaking Noah in Scene Seventeen*

ONE: DAVID

David You think, I must try not to think.

I must try not to think about it, if it is the it you think it might be.

You think you must not think of detail; dwell on detail. You must think the best. But then you find yourself, in a crowded street, glimpsing the back of a head far ahead, and your heart flutters and you think, no, it can't be, can it? But then you find you're thinking, but what if it is? What if it is and you're letting them go? So you accelerate, trying to dodge through the throng without barging anyone, or tripping over a child, or a buggy, and you're trying to keep glimpses of the back of the head, which has the same colour hair, to set a course by; and your breathing is high and fast, and your heart pumps, and you glimpse that they've entered a store, which you enter, after weaving across the flow of the throng, and people have said cross things at you in several languages and you've said sorry countless times, and excuse me almost as often; and you enter the store and reach the back of the head . . . And it isn't them, of course. It isn't her. Apart from the hair she isn't anything like her . . .

And that's the sort of thing you think when you're thinking the best. If you let your thoughts be thoughts of the worst you hear a river, and see a man's hands working under water. Pale, pale; bleached of colour.

Then your private detective informs you that Kevin Cross has a new girlfriend, and you say, girlfriend?! How has he acquired a girlfriend?

TWO: LETTERS

Kevin (*Fay's letter*) 'Dear Kevin Cross, I am Fay White, who used to live in Slindon. I saw you on the news. I haven't got anything to say, really, except to offer my address, if you want someone to write to.'

Fay (*Kevin's letter*) 'Dear Fay White, What a surprise to hear from you! Thank you for writing. I've often wondered what happened to you. It's a great comfort to know that someone from "back home" is thinking of me.'

Kevin (*Fay's letter*) 'So you are the Kevin Cross I used to know. That's the person I'm writing to, really. Perhaps that's the best way of looking at it. I can offer letters from someone who knew you before.'

Fay (*Kevin's letter*) 'I completely understand that you mustn't get involved in my appeal, but it's a good feeling, knowing that someone who knows me from before, the real me, is thinking of me. People who only know me from how I've been portrayed recently don't think well of me. It's a terrible thing to feel the world's against you. But you just have to get on with life. It's not what happens, but how you think about it.'

Kevin (*Fay's letter*) 'Dear Kevin, I've spoken to someone at the Home Office who's gone through the vetting process with me, and it sounds okay.'

THREE: GAOL

Fay waits, seated. Emile seats Kevin opposite her.

Emile No touching, no passing of objects, and all conversations to be conducted in English. Okay?

Emile moves away.

What Emile sees and hears of this and ensuing exchanges between Fay and Kevin is a matter for negotiation.

Fay and Kevin fidget.

Kevin Fancy a drink?

Fay I had a coffee.

Kevin I mean a real drink.

Fay ?

Kevin It was a joke.

Fay Sorry.

Kevin First time in one of these places?

Fay Yes.

Kevin Call me Kev, if you like. You haven't changed much.

Fay I haven't changed that much, have I? Apart from a bit of weight. I'm still basically the same Fay that I was.

Kevin Are you?

Fay Oh. You think I'm different. In what way do you think I'm different?

Kevin It's difficult to say.

Fay Go on. I'm interested.

Kevin Thanks for, um, writing.

It is you, isn't it? Fay White from Slindon.

Fay That's me.

Kevin Good. I wanted to be sure.

Yes, yes. It's you. It's the light in here. Hello, Fay White.

I'm in segregation. No one really talks to me. When was the last time you were in Slindon?

Fay Ages – years ago.

Kevin Me too.

Fay My mum moved.

Kevin Where to?

Fay Worthing.

Kevin Worthing, wow.

Fay Wow? You ever been there?

Kevin No.

Fay Thought you hadn't.

Kevin I need to know something, Fay.

I've been through it, you know. I'm still going through it. I'll come out the other side, that's for definite, but my faith in human beings has taken a knock, if not a kicking. I'm finding it hard to trust people . . .

He might weep. He shields his face.

Fay pushes a hanky across the table.

Emile What's that item!?

FOUR: DAVID

David And because, inexplicably, she's Kevin Cross's new girlfriend, you go to her address, and you wait, from a vantage point, until you see a woman who fits the description.

And you think, I know, I'll write her a letter, laying things out, in a way that I can. I can write and rewrite to get it right, what I'm saying.

But a letter, from a stranger, about something so personal
. . . So you think you'll have to approach her, friendly,
but how? In a city, how? How do you approach strangers,
females? You can say hello and they can say leave me
alone, or ignore you, or these days they can say fuck off.
So you think you're going to have to find a natural way
of placing yourself in a position where it appears natural
for you to talk with her. This woman called Fay. Find out
her hobby and take it up? What if it's badminton? You
loathe badminton. You hate everything about it. But you
can't take months over this. This is urgent. You need a
quick route to her. So you go to the private detective; the
one you're using anyway, and you ask them to investigate
her, that you want a way of approaching her naturally,
and you find, they find, she goes out of her home, she
goes to work in an office, she returns to her home.
Monday to Friday. She lives alone. She goes straight
home? She went to a park on the way home. She sat on a
bench and read a book. On the sixth day, the Saturday,
she went to the gaol again.

FIVE: GAOL

*Fay waits in an empty room. There's a table; a chair
either side of it.*

She waits a good while.

Enter Emile.

Emile You've had a wasted journey, I'm afraid. He can't
face it today. (*Offers envelope.*)

Fay Oh. (*The envelope's open.*) Oh.

Emile Had to be read. Sorry about that. I'll let you out
and you might be able to get a cup of tea.

SIX: DAVID

David Then she visited a bookshop, where she sat in various sofas on various floors reading various books. The private detective deduced that she did this on a regular basis. Sunday morning she got on a train, to Slough. Your private detective says he lost her, so you don't know what she did there. Okay, you think, on Monday morning, as well as everything else there is to do; to think, to not think; if the weather's fine tonight, you think, you're going to that park.

And it's very agreeable. Buds are budding. There's a little bit of warmth under the chill in the oncoming night air.

Enter Fay.

And she arrives at her bench, this Fay, and you watch, and wait, waiting for some chance or reason to speak with her . . .

And she takes out an envelope, and from the envelope she extracts paper, and reads words, and she smiles.

SEVEN: LETTER

Kevin Just a scribbled note to say I can't tell you how sorry I am about standing you up. What a waste of time for you. But I couldn't face it, I just couldn't. Please don't hate me. Look; I've written you a poem, by way of apologising.

EIGHT: DAVID

David And you think in a perfect world you'd be able to approach that smiling lady, doff your hat, if you wore one, and tell her how attractive her smile is and how her mood adds to the already delightful ambience in the park. But you can't do that; you might be able to if you were a very old man.

After a while there's nothing else for it but to sit on the same bench. At the other end, of course, and act as if you have no cause to dislike her.

When David sits, Fay's mood immediately changes. She might even go. David does as much as he can to be non-threatening. After a while Fay relaxes a little, risks a look at him. He's a late-middle-aged man. Safe? She puts away the envelope and takes out a novel.

It's spring, at last.

Fay continues reading.

I've a garden. Been out in it, tidying up, wondering what to do this year. Should I attempt anything major?

Fay doesn't look up.

I'm sorry. I'm interrupting your thoughts.

I've only a medium-sized garden. No willows like those. Or plane trees. And no silver birches. No trees at all. Treeless. Arboreally challenged. No leaves to rake in the autumn. No leaves for mulch.

Are you familiar with mulch?

No lake, either, nor pond, or any standing water, or flowing; no stream. Consequently, no ducks, or geese, or fish – are there any houses with streams near here? What about Her Majesty?

Never been invited?

You can visit Buckingham Palace in August.

If you pay. How much is it?

Takes out a pad and makes a note.

Memory like a sieve these days. I make notes of things
I want to remember – 'to do' lists – then I forget I made
them.

It says here, Christmas? That's it. That's the whole note.
What on earth does it refer to? I can't remember. Hard to
miss Christmas now that it starts in August. Some people
even buy their Christmas presents in the January sales. If
I bought my presents that early then I'd forget where I'd
put them. Or even that I'd bought them at all. And how
do you know who you're going to give what a year in
advance? All manner of events inevitably arise in the
course of a year. You buy a smart new lighter for a friend
and they give up smoking. Very wise, but your plan has
been thwarted. Anyway, whatever this Christmas note to
myself referred to must have been unimportant, or
accomplished, if only inadvertently. My name's David. I
have to say, I couldn't help noticing, what a lovely smile
you have. Is it all right for me to say that, I mean at my
age?

I couldn't fail to miss your smile.

You're reading? What pleasure, to read.

You read novels. What pleasure. What worlds. Worlds of
words.

There you are, in a bookshop. You pick up a tome,
at random, or something draws you to it, the covers,
these days, quite possibly, or it's a title you know a little
about –

Fay stops reading.

– or an author you've read, and you're in a bookshop,
but then you open the book, read a few words and you're
off! Off somewhere, with someone. Can you beat that?
Can you?

Fay I know what you mean.

David You do?

Fay Yes.

David What a thing an engrossing novel is.

Fay I try not to think of how many I shan't be able to read.

David Lack of time, you mean?

Fay I could read one in a day when I was a kid.

David A thick one?

Fay Not a thick one, no. I read *Jane Eyre* in a day.

David That must have been summer holidays or somesuch.

Fay Or 'somesuch', yes.

David I was a bit of a bookworm, too, for a few months, once upon a time. Had to take extended bed rest. Rheumatic fever. Don't get it here, now. Antibiotics. You haven't suffered a long illness, I hope?

Fay No.

David Good. I'm glad to hear it. Have you ever before met anyone who's had rheumatic fever?

Fay Not that I know of.

David The increase in identification and treatment of disease is one of the incontestable signs that we are progressing, don't you think?

Fay Yes.

David One day we'll know everything about everything, do you think?

Fay I don't know.

David Maybe that will spell the end of the novel. When we know for a fact what goes on in the human mind and heart. When we can know what motivates others to perpetrate the inexplicable. Should we all write a novel about ourselves?

Fay Would that be a novel?

David Someone write one about us, then?

Fay A biography?

David No, I don't mean a record of who, what and where, I mean something about us, something that captures us, the why of us.

Fay An explanation.

David Then others could read it. We, for instance, meeting like this for the first time, could exchange the novels that have been written about us, and read them, and then we'd know each other much better, and have a broad knowledge to draw on whilst becoming acquainted. Even, perhaps, we could read our own novels written about us, and so know ourselves much better, and perhaps effect change.

Fay I'd like that.

Can you choose who writes the novel about you?

David Ah. Now this could be a very good game.

Fay Too revealing.

David Go on.

Fay Your choice will be interpreted as an indication of how you think of yourself. If I said I wanted – and we must be able to include dead writers – Virginia Woolf to write me – then you would think that I saw life, the world, in her tones; that I had a tendency towards melancholy. But if I said I wanted J. K. Rowling to write me, you might think that I live in a fantasy world, with all that that entails.

David What does that entail?

David's inadvertently let something slip that Fay picks up on.

Fay Keeping an eye out for trolls.

David Trolls, ah yes. My daughter had one on the end of her pencil. Which novelist would I choose? I don't know. George MacDonald Fraser, then I'd be roguish, appear not to care too deeply about anything, have lots of scrapes and lots of exotic women.

Fay Where do you live?

David Is something the matter?

Fay How often do you come to this park?

David This is the very first time.

It seems Fay might leave, but then she doesn't.

David has a thermos flask. He pours a hot drink and offers it. Fay declines.

You're a regular here?

I like travelling a few stops. See where I'm drawn to.

Fay's suddenly walking away.

Fay It's starting to rain.

David Oh . . .

Goodbye.

Fay Goodbye.

David It's been a pleasure meeting you.

He looks up to the sky. There are indeed a few drops of rain. He sips his drink.

NINE: GAOL

The scene is under way when we join it.

Emile monitors.

Fay Thanks for the poem.

Kevin Oh, that.

Fay It's very special. I mean, it makes me smile. And . . .

Kevin And what?

Fay That's it. It makes me smile.

Kevin What sort of smile?

Fay . . . Pleasure.

Kevin What sort of pleasure?

Fay I'm going to try to write you one back.

Kevin I'm wondering whether I shouldn't have written it. Or if I should have written it but not sent it.

Fay Oh no, no, no. I'm glad you did.

Kevin It feels a bit silly in the cold light of day.

You look like you still have the boys chasing after you. Why would you want a poem from me?

The man you settled down with is a lucky guy.

Fay The boys might still indeed be chasing after me.

Kevin So you're not married?

Fay Would you have sent me that poem if I was?

Kevin A string of boyfriends, then, with you playing hard to get?

Fay Not a string, no.

Kevin Fay White was the prettiest, sexiest girl in the village. You were the benchmark, the gold standard. We boys divvied ourselves up into who you might go out with and who you wouldn't touch with a bargepole.

Fay Well, we were getting somewhere.

Kevin And then we didn't.

Fay Anita Smith.

Kevin This is it. Anita Smith; a precocious talent.

You were far too classy to go anywhere Anita Smith had been.

Fay I was classy, wasn't I?

Kevin Still are.

Fay Thank you, kind sir.

Kevin My pleasure.

That smile, that twinkle in the eyes; that hasn't changed.

He might have gone too far.

How's your mum?

Fay She's okay. Still in Worthing. What about yours?

Kevin Dead, thankfully. I don't know how she'd cope with all this. And Dad's disowned me. As if I care. He was always –

Emile No touching! Hands to yourself. Rules broken. Visit terminated.

Kevin What?

Emile Rules!

Emile manoeuvres Kevin out.

Kevin (*extempore*)
If I knew now, what I knew then
I'd never have walked away like I did.
Now meeting you in my time of strife
Has given me hope in my life.

Thank you Fay,
You went away
But now you're back a ray
Of sunshine has lighted my day.

Emile Pam Ayres eat your heart out.

TEN: DAVID

David You see her exit the gaol, visibly upset. What do
you feel? Do you feel for her? Well, yes. You've met her.
Despite what you know of her it was not unpleasant. She
is easy on the eye.

The next day you take up a vantage point outside her
place of work. When she exits, alone, you try to follow
her, but she's too quick on her feet for you, and, in the
crowded street you lose her. So you head for the park,
but she's not there. The private detective gave you her
mobile phone number, which, for a moment, you consider
dialling; to say what? I was trying to follow you but I lost
you, so please retrace your steps so I can try again?

ELEVEN: BOOKSHOP

Fay is on a sofa, reading. Enter David. He sits on the sofa. Fay stares at him. He tries to pretend he's surprised it's her.

David Hello!

Fay Hello?

David Looking for the novelist to write you?

Fay No.

David The word coincidence is playing in your mind. But we might have been here at the same time numerous times and never known. You're thinking coincidence, but shall I tell you a coincidence that makes us meeting here pale into insignificance?

Fay No.

David All right; let me talk, let me tell you. I come from a family that's in anguish. Look, I don't mean any harm, we're in a public place, so please hear me out –

Fay If it's not a coincidence you're here, then how did you find me, how did you know where I'd be?

David Well, I followed you –

Fay Followed me from where?

David From, from your place of work –

Fay You know where I work?

David I'm not any threat too you, I assure you.

Fay Why do you know all this about me?

David I know it might seem odd and confusing and baffling and even alarming that a man comes up to you and it transpires that he seems to know –

Fay You tell me right now who you are and what you wa—

David This is quite hard because we're now attracting a lot of attention –

Fay Good –

David And what I have to tell you is quite intricate –

Exit Fay.

Beats.

Enter Fay.

Fay Do you know where I live?

David Yes.

Fay And my name?

What the fuck are you up to?

David Katherine Desouza.

Fay ?

David Kevin Cross is a friend of yours, I believe.

Fay Ahh. What are you – police? No – journalist? Lawyer?

Whatever, this has been what – an attempt at some sort of entrapment?

What's your real name? What's your real whole name?

David It is David. I'm really called David. David Desouza.

Look, here, these are my credit cards, and a business card, and a travelcard. Here, have a card. I'm just an ordinary man –

Fay If I ever see you again I'll have you arrested. In fact, I'll arrest you myself.

Exit Fay.

David nearly shouts something after her.

He sits back in the sofa. He picks up a book for something to do. He waits for the shop to return to normal. He tries not to appear too upset.

His mobile phone rings. He looks at it. There's no caller ID.

David Hello?

Fay comes into view. She's watching him.

Hello?

Fay ends the call.

TWELVE: LETTERS

David Dear Fay White, I am writing to apologise for startling you so badly today. Katherine Desouza is my daughter. She has been missing for just coming up to two years, now. If you are familiar with Kevin Cross and his case, you might recognise her name from the margins.

Fay (*continuing David's letter to her*) 'All I was seeking to do was to find out from you if you or Kevin could be of any help to us in ascertaining what has happened to Katherine. Myself, her husband and her young son live in hope that she shall be returned to us, but, failing that, it would be an enormous relief just to know what, if anything, has happened to her.'

David (*Fay's letter to him*) 'Dear Mr Desouza, You write as if you are an honest man, but of course you are not, otherwise you would have been upfront with me rather than trying to trick me.'

Kevin Dear Fay, From my cell I can hear a bird singing at dusk. I think it's a blackbird, but I never went in for wild life. It reminds me of the village, and I imagine that when the bird flies away from me, it flies to you, and perches on a tree by your window, and sings to you.

Fay (*continuing Kevin's letter*) 'So give it a message for me, and I'll give it one for you. Oops, a bit suggestive. So give it a message for me, and I'll do the same.'

Kevin (*Fay's letter to him*) 'Dear Kevin, There is indeed a blackbird that sings outside my window. It sings so sweetly. I often think that people like us should never have come to London. I keep on thinking of going home, but that could be a big mistake. Better to go somewhere new and start all over again. I've been through it, too. I left Slindon, came here to "make it". Took a knock, then another. Woke up one day – huh? How did I end up here?'

Dear Fay, Far better to go somewhere new. Far better to start again, to slough off old skins. My lawyer, Mr Bullock, says still no sign of the chief witness. Michael Penn obviously did a deal because he's no longer in gaol. I beg Mr Bullock to get on with finding him. We'll get him in the dock, and we'll nail him and the truth. And I have nightmares. What if Michael Penn went after you? He's sick enough.

Emile (*continuing Kevin's letter to Fay*) 'Don't walk near the Thames, Fay. Promise me that you won't walk near the river. P.S. The blackbird sang me to sleep last evening.'

David Dear Fay, Thank you for your letter. I am aware that Kevin Cross protests his innocence of the crimes attributed to so-called 'John the Baptist' – however, the place at which Katherine was last known to be is inside the geographical profile of John the Baptist, and so I wonder, as Kevin has admitted or been shown to be familiar with that area, whether he might be able to provide any information, no matter how seemingly insignificant, to help us understand Katherine's disappearance.

THIRTEEN: GAOL

Fay is waiting, seated. Emile delivers Kevin.

Emile stands right by the table, dominating.

Fay looks up at him.

Emile doesn't move.

Fay might speak out, but Kevin gives a little shake of his head.

Emile moves away.

Kevin Sorry.

Fay Not your fault.

Kevin Thanks for your poem . . . Don't be embarrassed. Didn't you mean it?

Fay I didn't write it. I copied it.

Kevin You didn't write it?

Fay No.

Kevin Oh.

Fay I couldn't have written that. It's too good.

Kevin Did you try to write something?

Fay Yes, but it was no good.

Kevin A poem?

Fay I wouldn't call it a poem. The one I sent you's a poem.

Kevin I bet you could write one as good as that.

Fay No.

Kevin I bet you could . . .

What's up?

Fay There was a blackbird this morning.

Kevin Did it sing you a message?

Fay It was singing.

Kevin I sent it. I think about you a lot. What might have been.

How many men have asked you out this week?

Fay None. I've been thinking about where other people might be now.

Kevin People from home?

Fay Anita Smith left.

Kevin I think she had to, what with her reputation.

Fay That's the trouble for us girls.

Kevin What is?

Fay We have to be careful.

Kevin I'm not judging Anita. If I'd've loved her I'd've settled down with her and to hell with what people said. But I didn't love her.

There's no news on Michael Penn.

None.

Mr Bullock says that what with the Freedom of Information Act the police'll have to divulge if there's been any deal with him. Mr Bullock's great. I think. He was mental after the verdict. He kept on saying, 'How can they believe Michael Penn? How can they believe him? Fucking juries!' I told him I could understand the jury believing Michael Penn because I believed him once. That night we shared a cell I believed he was a nice bloke. I worry about you coming to see me. Michael Penn's sick, you know.

Fay He must have known you were vulnerable; that you were familiar with that part of the river.

Kevin 'That part of the river' is a quarter of a mile long, Fay.

Fay But you don't live there, and you don't work there, and you –

Kevin What is this, Fay?

Fay These are the sorts of questions I'm going to be asked –

Kevin By who? Who's asking you these sorts of questions, Fay? . . .

Is it yourself asking yourself these sorts of questions?

Fay I'm trying to establish the details that meant a miscarriage of justice was possible, Kev. Certain things led the police to you –

Kevin The man who should be sitting here led them to me! We shared a cell for one lousy night! And I shouldn't have even been there. Me and effing Michael Penn had a right good heart-to-heart, I thought, but what he was actually doing was pumping me and when he found out that I knew that stretch of the river he must have thought, bingo! Here's my fall guy. And off he toddles to stitch me up. I tell you, once the police get something in their heads, it's a bastard to shift.

Fay But you were vulnerable. Michael Penn couldn't have pointed the finger at me, for instance.

Kevin Are there any female serial killers killing women?

Fay It's a shame you didn't have any alibis.

Kevin Single man . . .

Fay No girlfriend?

Kevin No.

Fay No Anita Smiths?

Kevin Well, you know, the odd flurry. You never been married?

Fay I was living with someone, once. We did get married. It's over.

Kevin What happened?

Fay He left me.

Kevin He must be mad . . . What?

Fay That's when I understood Miss Havisham.

Kevin Miss who?

Fay Cobwebs everywhere and the curtains shut. That's me. The woman who never recovers from being jilted.

Kevin This bloke never jilted you, did he?

Fay No.

Kevin I was married, actually.

Fay I read that you were.

Kevin The ex-wife from hell is in Australia now, with her latest conquest. My daughter's there, too.

Fay You've a daughter?

Kevin Simone. She's seven.

Fay Do you . . . do they ever come home?

Kevin Australia's her home. When this is all over I'm going to fight custody.

Well, I'll see.

Fay Wasn't that sorted out before they went?

Kevin No. The police said that my failed marriage was a motive for being John the Baptist. I said that my ex-wife was indeed the cause of it all, because she falsely accused me and I was arrested and on remand and that's when I met Michael Penn, and now I'm here, and she dropped the charges after I was charged with being John the Baptist because she'd got what she wanted – me in the shit, but her false accusations still stuck in the police's minds and formed part of their case against me, and if every justifiably pissed-off ex-husband went on the rampage there'd be dead women everywhere, more than there are now – I know there are lots of dead women, lots and lots – there's a war on terror but not one on woman-killing.

Sorry, that sounds horrible.

We should be having a war on woman-killing, that's what we should be having a war on. It's a disgrace.

I said to the police, if I wanted to kill my ex-wife I'd've killed her, not five prostitutes, like John the Baptist.

Fay They weren't all prostitutes, were they?

Kevin Maybe he thought they were all prostitutes. Three of them were.

Fay You think he wanted to kill prostitutes, then?

Kevin I don't know what he wanted. I only know what he did.

Fay His behaviour can't be completely random otherwise there wouldn't be any sort of pattern, any geographical profile to John the Baptist.

Kevin That geographical profile was drawn up from the ones they know about. But if there were other crimes outside the geographical profile, then it would change to include them.

Fay You think there's more, then?

Kevin He's out there.

Fay Maybe he'll stop now, because if he strikes again it'll prove it wasn't you and they'll reopen the case.

Kevin I try not to think like that. I try not to think that the death of some poor woman could be to my advantage. You're up to speed with my case.

Fay I went to the library.

Kevin Checking up on me?

There's a day I keep thinking of. Back home. I'd got my first car. The Escort. Feeling full of myself, I pull up next to you on Stone Road. You were walking alone with your nose in a book, weren't you? To my surprise – and delight – you get in. It was hot. I had Bruce Springsteen playing. 'The River'. We went down by the Sow. We were being coy. I was shitting myself. Fay White! Got in my car! Sat by me on the river bank! (*Sings.*) 'We'd go down by the river, and into the river we'd dive.' We had a little kiss, if I remember rightly.

Fay Little?

Kevin A good long kiss. In the sun.

Fay I wanted you to put your hands up my top, inside my bra.

Kevin You never!

Fay I did.

Kevin Gulp.

Why didn't you say?

Fay I didn't know if you wanted to.

Kevin Wanted to?! I could hardly think straight! I was being blessed by the closest thing to a princess Slindon village ever had. If only I'd known! If only I'd known that! My hand in your bra? On my list of things I wish I'd known, that goes straight in at number one. If I'd've known that, there's no way I would have let Anita Smith turn my head.

Fay From what I heard, Kevin, she didn't turn your head, she gave you head.

    Beats.

Kevin You always could be a bit of a naughty girl, couldn't you?

Fay Not naughty enough.

Kevin Naughty enough now, I bet.

Fay That was a golden day.

Kevin But it could have been platinum. If I'd have got my hand in your bra that afternoon, there's no way Anita Smith would have got a look in.

If only I'd known!

Fay We could go back there one day.

Kevin I'd like that. I'd like that very much. That thought will help me to keep going.

Fay And me. There haven't been many days like that. Golden days. I can smell it all. You were a bit of a catch –

Kevin Me?

Fay With your low car –

Kevin – dropped suspension –

Fay – with shiny wheels –

Kevin – chrome –

Fay – and your muscles and your eyes and your smile.

Emile One minute.

Kevin What?

Emile One minute.

Kevin You're having a laugh.

Emile I will be soon. I'll be off shift, in the bar. Finish up.

Kevin We've got more time.

Emile We're short-staffed. Someone might have come along to relieve me, but they haven't.

Kevin She's come all this w—

Emile You're wasting your minute.

Fay It's all right, Kev, I don't mind.

Kevin Well, I do.

Fay I don't want you to get into trouble.

Kevin (*extempore*)
My golden day with Fay
I thought I'd lost for good
But there's going to be another –

Emile
I was down by the river wearing a hood
When I saw her I got wood
But rather than pulling my pud
I killed her.

Back to your cell, Pam. Stay seated, please, miss. I'll be two ticks.

Emile manoeuvres Kevin out.

32

Kevin Stay strong, Fay.

Emile
Fay, Fay,
Don't go away,
I'll return
Without delay.
Come on, Pam,
Me and you could have a poetry slam
One evening.

Kevin I'll send the blackbird!

Exit Emile and Kevin.

Fay waits.

Enter Emile. He studies Fay.

Emile Thank you for waiting.

Fay You have to let me out so I didn't have any choice.

Emile
Fay, Fay,
Stay away.

Fay
Nay, nay,
No way.
I'll return
Another day.

Emile opens his mouth to speak.

Whatever you say.

FOURTEEN: LETTER

David Dear Fay, Is it the drama? We all like a bit of drama. He's in gaol, he's been on the news, you're bored . . . No?

Or it's your perfect relationship. You visit him in there, somebody tells you when and for how long you can see him, you don't have to make any decisions, you don't have to go food-shopping together, you don't have to discuss bills or what to watch on telly or . . . all that stuff. And you leave him, every time. And you know where he is all the time. Dear Fay, are you a control freak? . . .

Or do you like bad men? Do you find violence sexually arousing? I'm sorry, you don't have to answer that – in fact, I'm sorry I asked. I don't want to know the answer . . .

Do you really believe Kevin is innocent?

I'm prepared to listen . . .

Dear Fay, please help me.

FIFTEEN: BOOKSHOP

Fay I asked to meet because I recognise that your anguish is genuine and I believe in doing the right things in life, so I will try to help you. I've seen Kevin again and I have to tell you that Kevin's lawyer believes that the convictions against him are unsafe. It is Kevin's lawyer's belief that Michael Penn, whose testimony about Kevin's confession was about the only evidence the police had, should himself be investigated.

David Thank you.

I have heard the suggestion that Michael Penn is indeed himself the perpetrator.

Fay I was very careful not to say that, exactly. But there appears to have been some sort of deal struck, because he's not in gaol any more.

David Indeed he isn't.

Fay Anyway. (*She's going.*)

David You're right, there's no forensic evidence at all, just Michael Penn's statement about Kevin's confession – and the CCTV footage, of Kevin, in the vicinity, the night my daughter disappeared. Did you know about that?

Fay Anyone could have been 'in the vicinity' – in fact nine other men were, and four women.

David They've all been eliminated and Kevin's never been able to satisfactorily explain why he's seen running away.

Fay There are two points there. I'll take them in turn. One: he was running away from an attempted mugging. Two: 'they've all been eliminated' from what, because there was no known crime committed 'in the vicinity'?

David That's what he claims. About the mugging, I mean.

Fay What proof have you that he wasn't fleeing a mugging?

David Why do you think Kevin's almost universally disbelieved?

Fay I don't think that he is. And anyway, most people don't really think for themselves, do they? We run in packs. It takes a strong individual to stand aside and say, 'You're all wrong.'

David That's you, is it; the 'strong individual'?

Fay I'm not involved in his appeal.

David You're defending him to me.

Fay I'm just stating the case.

David Do you know Kevin's ex-wife?

Fay I didn't see Kevin for several years, so no.

David So you've only recently been in touch.

Fay Since I saw about his case.

David I see.

Since his arrest, or since his conviction?

Fay Kevin wasn't charged with anything in connection with your daughter, was he?

David No. But her clothing, a piece of her clothing, was found on the river bank within John the Baptist's geographical profile.

Fay The piece of clothing obviously doesn't tie Kevin to your daughter or it'd be evidence. She might have dropped it by accident.

David Unlikely. It was her bra.

Fay Oh . . .

David What do you mean, 'Oh'? You think she might have chosen to undress at night by that stretch of the Thames?

Fay Well, I don't know her, so I can't say.

David No, you can't. As you said, you can't say, or imply, or infer.

Fay I didn't mean anything bad when I said 'Oh'.

David This is a photograph of her with my son-in-law, and their son.

36

Fay looks.

Impossible to know what to tell him.

Do you read James Ellroy?

Fay I didn't have you as an James Ellroy kind of guy. Ah. I see. James Ellroy's mother.

David His quest to find her killer.

Fay But she definitely was killed.

David But he doesn't know who killed her.

Fay Whereas you think you know who killed your daughter, even though she might not be dead.

David Her son, my grandson's, called Freddy. What to tell Freddy?

Fay What does he believe now?

David He's only three. We stall him. He doesn't know how to measure time, he doesn't know when too much time has passed for an explanation to be implausible. I have to ask you, Fay, do you believe that the murders Kevin's convicted of were committed by one man?

Fay Yes, I do believe that.

David Do you think you can take a man who does those things and improve him to the point that he stops doing them?

And how can you tell if you have?

You can't generally identify a sadistic murderer from their appearance. But that's a strange thing, isn't it? You see photos of Fred West and you think, of course he's a sadistic murderer! But people looked at him every day without deducing his nature.

In the same way that you can look at Kevin Cross even now –

37

Fay It's not the same way, is it?

David Some people look at him and see a sadistic murderer who raped women with a screwdriver whilst you see someone else entirely.

Fay No one knows for certain that it was a screwdriver.

David One man does.

You're well up on the case.

Fay I'm not thick, you know.

David Are you religious at all?

Fay No.

David The use of the 'John the Baptist' soubriquet has always struck me as distasteful.

Fay I think it's meant to be ironic.

David I can understand how puzzling it must be to know someone then find them accused of terrible crimes. Even if you haven't seen them for several years. The disbelief must be profound. I remember when Katherine, aged ten, was accused of being part of a gang who beat up another girl at school. I was furious with the school for being so stupid as to believe that my daughter would do such a thing. I spent the night sleepless, fuming, fantasising about how I would avenge her honour.

But she'd done it.

She saw the mood I was in as we approached the school and she confessed to me.

Fay You liked your daughter so you believed her, you dislike Kevin so you believe he's guilty –

David No, I believe he's guilty, therefore I dislike him.

Fay You think I'm a fool. Or a twat.

David I don't walk in your shoes so I can only speculate.

Fay You do think I'm a twat, though.

David Not a word I'd use.

My wife died after Katherine disappeared. She'll never know the answer – well, she might. Who knows what the dead know? Only the dead themselves. We were divorced, anyway.

Fay Oh?

David Which has got nothing to do with anything.

Fay I only said, 'Oh'.

David No, it was 'Oh?' There was a question –

Fay Have you followed any women before?

David What?

Fay Have you?

David No, I haven't –

Fay Have you?

David Fuck off.

Fay That's no way to speak to me.

David Fuck off. I've had it up to here!

Fay I will fuck off, then. (*leaving*) You found me, I didn't find you.

David Please . . . We'd give anything to know. I can't say that Kevin Cross is definitely, beyond all doubt, John the Baptist, I can see how it might be that he isn't, but he was in the vicinity of my daughter's last known whereabouts, and he might know something, anything, that could shed light on her disappearance.

Exit Fay.

SIXTEEN: DAVID

David Sunday, you nip off and wait for Fay at the station from which trains embark for Slough. You follow her onto the train.

You've never been to Slough before. Then there it is. This is Slough . . . What can you say? It's a place.

You follow her off the train, through some streets, and you begin to ask yourself what are you doing here, following her here? How can you explain this? What do you hope to achieve? Have you become what is known as a stalker? Have you slipped into abnormal, disturbed behaviour without realising? And she enters what you learn is a hospital . . . You go in through one door, and nobody stops you. At the end of a corridor you see thick doors. Someone exits them using a code. You know you'd have trouble getting in there. To the side you see more doors, not so thick. Less daunting. People pass through without having to punch a code. You go through. A female, a nurse, near a desk, says hello. You say hello in return and you concoct a story on the spot. You've just returned to this country, a family member is supposed to be meeting you here. You're a bit hazy. Jet lag. The family member is called Fay White. Ah yes, you're told, she's visiting Noah. You're given directions. You follow them, following the room numbers. Before the one, you stop, and look around you, then slowly peer into the room. You glimpse the back of her; the side of a young man, comatose.

SEVENTEEN: HOSPITAL

Noah is sitting back in his chair, heavily sedated. He makes the occasional tiny movement but never any sound.

Fay sits next to him. She leans in.

Fay Hellooooo. Hellooooo. How are we? How are we?

Satisfied that he isn't going to respond, Fay sits back.

Beats.

Fay takes out a novel.

She opens it.

She takes out another. She reads. She closes it. She begins to read the first.

She shows Noah the cover as if for his approval.

This isn't it. It's good, but it's not it.

She reads for a few moments. She gives up.

Noah?

I'll still come and see you, but I'm drawn to a man who makes me laugh.

Fay watches Noah for a long time, as if for a response.

He's from my heyday.

When I was special.

Fay kisses Noah's cheek.

David It's an intensely private moment. You feel disgusted with yourself.

Interval.

NINETEEN: GAOL

Fay waits, seated.

Enter Emile.

Emile We're running late. Sorry. Did they search you properly?

Fay Yes.

Emile The full intimate?

Fay Yes.

Emile She's a dyed-in-the-wool lesbian, the one who does it. Loves her work.

What are these, I hear you cry? These are letters, from women, to your boyfriend. He's been writing back.

Shall I get him?

Exit Emile.

Fay hums 'The River' under her breath.

Enter Emile and Kevin, who's very down. It's a difficult walk for Kevin because his trousers are too small for him.

Emile moves away.

Kevin won't look at Fay.

Fay Kevin?

Kevin Look at my fucking trousers!

Fay They do look a bit uncomfortable.

Kevin Just when they were about to bring me up, laundry comes and leaves me with these. Deliberate. A niggle. Because you were coming.

Fay I see.

Kevin What's funny, Fay? What could possibly be funny?

Fay I wouldn't worry too much. They're only slightly tighter than the ones you used to wear in the old days.

Kevin I was a bit trimmer then.

What a smile. What a smile.

Fay You're smiling now. Good.

Kevin Actually, another reason why they're messing me about with my trousers is that Mr Bullock's come up with something.

Fay What's he come up with?

Kevin He's driven a bus through one of Michael Penn's alibis, is all.

Fay Fantastic!

Kevin It's great, isn't it? Now he's really got to track Michael Penn down. And we're following up any interest in me – enquiries from television people, campaigning journalists and all that – I've been writing to – there's a programme I've found out about – I'm made for it – all they'd have to do is show me, show Michael Penn – destroy that alibi – and then the world will know the truth. He managed to pull the wool over the eyes of the police and that jury but most people, most normal people would know, if they saw us, that he's a liar – I tell you, I have dreams about – not dreams – I'm awake – I have fantasies about – the only thing I feel thankful for is that I'm in gaol somewhere that hasn't got the death penalty – imagine what it's like when you're not only fighting for justice but fighting for your life – how can it be possible in a so-called civilised country that I'm in here purely on the lies of a criminal? I wake up drenched in sweat – I have this nightmare that I'm being lynched – but it's not just a nightmare because I have been lynched metaphorically in real life, but instead of it being over in a few minutes it's going on and on and . . .

Fay I don't know what it must be like for you.

Kevin It's indescribable.

Fay But people get through it.

Kevin I don't know how.

Fay You're fighting despair –

Kevin It's winning –

Fay – and your trousers.

Kevin That's funny but not funny, Fay.

Fay I know. You're trying hard not to smile. Give in.

Kevin There. I'm smiling.

Fay There's a couple of books I can send you –

Kevin Is one called *Attack of the Killer Trousers*?

Fay Novels. About people who've got through it. Who've been falsely imprisoned. One's *A Day in the Life of Ivan Denisovich* by Alexander Solzhenitsyn.

Kevin Bloody hell.

Fay He was imprisoned in a Soviet Gulag, for dissent.

Kevin I'm not the world's greatest reader, Fay.

Fay You write poems.

Kevin Poems are short.

Fay This is a short novel. Only this thick.

Kevin I'm not sure.

Fay I'll send it. Have a look at it . . .

Have other people been writing to you?

Kevin A few.

Fay Women?

Kevin A few. Why do you ask?

Fay Just taking an interest.

Kevin catches Fay's involuntary glance to Emile.

Kevin Fay?

Fay What?

Kevin I know you well enough by now to know when something's wrong.

Fay There's nothing wrong.

Kevin Are you jealous?

Fay Have you met any of them?

Kevin I haven't taken out a lonely hearts ad, you know. They just write to me.

Fay What do they say?

Kevin You know. Nothing really.

Fay They say nothing?

Kevin They introduce themselves.

Fay So you don't know any of them?

Kevin None of them.

Fay What do they write?

'Hello, Kevin, I'm Jenny from Nottingham and I'm a size twelve and I like going out to the pictures and horse riding.'

Kevin That sort of thing.

Some of them say that they feel that I'm innocent. They want to know if there's an official campaign to free me. One wants to start one.

Some of them are a bit sick.

Fay Oh?

Kevin The ones who say that the victims must have deserved it.

Fay They say that?

Kevin In so many words.

Fay Have you replied to any of these women?

Kevin Yes.

Fay How many?

Kevin All of them.

Fay Even the sick ones?

Kevin Especially them, to tell them to examine their hearts.

Fay What about the non-sick ones?

Kevin I just reply in the same way they wrote to me. Tell them a bit about myself.

Fay Do you tell any of them about me?

Kevin Do I what?

Fay Do you say anything about me?

Kevin Why should I tell a stranger about my private life? It wouldn't feel right.

What?

Fay It's okay.

Kevin Have you talked to any men out there?

Fay Not really.

Kevin 'Not really.'

You're making me feel like I've done something wrong, Fay.

Fay I haven't talked to any men.

Kevin None?

Fay I went to see Noah.

Kevin Noah?

Fay The ex I told you about. In hospital.

Kevin Hospital?

Fay Yes.

Kevin What's wrong with him?

Fay They don't really know.

Kevin Have you told him about me?

Fay I have, actually.

Kevin What did you tell him about me?

Fay That you make me laugh.

Kevin What did Noah say?

Fay He doesn't speak.

When he's like that.

Kevin It's bad, then.

Fay He's in a mental hospital.

Kevin I see. I'm sorry.

Fay They don't know what it is.

Kevin It's good of you to visit your ex. You're a good person.

Someone telling you about the letters I get; these trousers – they're trying to split us up.

One of the things that's kept me going, is thinking about what you said, about you wanting me to stick my hand in your bra. (*Sings.*) 'Down by the river, and into the river we dived.' I'm finding my imagination is running wild. Silky-smooth skin, then a sudden nipple.

Emile Sit back, both of you.

They do, defiantly.

Kevin Have I allowed any other women in here?

Emile It's not a question of you allowing them; we allow them, we decide if they're allowed – sit down, Cross –

Kevin Have any other –

Emile Sit down!

Kevin Have any other women been here?

Emile No!

Kevin (*sits*) Thank you.

Emile moves away. Then moves back.

Emile Would we let a child visit a convicted paedophile? No, of course we wouldn't. (*to Fay*) You're being groomed.

Fay I'm here because I want to be.

Emile moves away, smiling.

Kevin Twat . . .

You're the only woman who's sat where you are, Fay. Some of the women who've written to me . . . I think it gives some of them a thrill.

Fay I'm not one of them, Kevin –

Kevin I know you're not –

Fay But I have found that being associated with you has made people take an interest in me.

Kevin Oh?

Fay A man called David Desouza.

Kevin Oh.

The bloke with the daughter.

Fay He found me.

Kevin Found you?

Fay He followed me.

Kevin David Desouza followed you?

Have you reported him?

Fay He's not like that.

Kevin How do you know?

Fay He's okay.

Kevin How do you know?

Fay I've talked to him a few times.

Kevin You should be careful who you talk to.

Fay He found me!

Kevin Just be careful, that's all . . . Did he tell you much about his daughter?

Fay Just her name. And about the footage you're both in, but I'd read about that.

Kevin He didn't tell you that she'd tried suicide before.

Fay No.

Kevin Well, she did. I've never been charged with anything to do with her, you know? The police just scooped up everything that might ever have happened in that area and tried to pin it on me. David Desouza's written to me. Several times. I feel really, genuinely sorry for the man. But I've told him, I wrote back to him – yes, me and her appear in footage from the same CCTV, but we're not together. We're minutes apart. I didn't see her. I've told him that I can't help him. I didn't see her. What about all the other men in that footage?

Fay Okay –

Kevin I didn't see her, but if I did and I say that I saw her that night down there they're just going to say that I killed her. They're not going to treat me as a witness, are they? David Desouza's on the other side, as far as I'm concerned. I feel sorry for him, but he's on the other side. He thinks I killed his daughter.

Beats.

Fay It was a golden day, our day by the river.

Kevin Wasn't it? I'm so sorry I went off with Anita Smith that night.

Fay I was gutted; but it was my fault. I should have made my desires known.

Kevin 'Desires'.

Fay Are you sure we were listening to 'The River'?

Kevin Whaddya mean?

Fay Nothing, Kevin. Just wondering.

Kevin It was 'The River'. We lay by the River Sow, listening to 'The River' . . . It really frightens me when you doubt me. I get scared. It's so fucking lonely in here.

David Desouza's sent me maps, showing my 'possible routes that night', picked out in different colours. With his daughter's 'possible routes' picked out in other colours. All the permutations. With 'possible timings'.

What does he look like?

Fay He's (*brief description of actor playing David*).

Kevin He's ——— and ——— ? And what build?

Fay A (bit/much lighter/heavier) than you.

Kevin And how's he speak – where's he from?

Fay replies accordingly.

Fucking hell, Fay.

Fay What?

Kevin Are you sure he's David Desouza?

Fay Am I what? Yes! Yes!

Kevin How did you meet him – tell me exactly.

Fay I told you – he followed me. Then he introduced himself.

Kevin Were you near the river?

Fay No, nowhere near it.

Kevin So he said he was David Desouza?

Fay Yes!

Kevin And have you checked that?

Fay Checked it? No, but I rang his number and he answered – I saw him.

Kevin What number?

Fay His mobile.

Kevin How did you get his mobile number?

Fay?

Fay?

Fay He gave me his mobile number.

Emile Time, lady and not-so-gentleman. Time –

Fay What is it, Kev? What is it – you're scaring me!

Emile Time.

Kevin Fucking hell, Fay – you don't know who this bloke really is and that description you gave fits Michael Penn!

Emile Time!

Fay Michael Penn?

Kevin Promise me that you'll –

Emile Time!

Fay I don't think it's Michael Penn – I really don't – I –

Emile Time.

> *Emile manoeuvres Kevin away, leaving Fay alone. Sound effects of keys, doors. More keys and doors. They go on, beyond reality; each sound like a little blow to Fay's head.*

TWENTY: FAY

Fay Address on card and mobile and landline. He gave me. Stake out address. Must be his – I wrote him there, he wrote back. Proof it's him? No.

Get there, phone his landline. Say I want to meet. Now. I want to meet now! In bookshop. He comes out of address, hurrying. Landline matches address and he gets mail there . . . but whose house?

Internet café. Electoral roll. Register to use. Buy credits. Input name, address. Yes. David Desouza registered there. That is him . . . Proof?

Is it? Still not proof that he actually is David Desouza.

Google Michael Penn. No photos. Not one fucking photo! Google David Desouza. No photo! . . .

This is hysteria, this is paranoia. That man is David Desouza. Must be.

Text him. Running late. That is David Desouza. Gut feeling. Man with troubled daughter. Disappeared. Latched onto Kevin. Some end of story better than no end. Poor man.

TWENTY-ONE: BOOKSHOP

Fay Bookshop; spy on him. Looking around for me.

I know; ask assistant to page him, then watch his reaction. Watch him when name called.

Assistant can't page unless lost child – Oh . . . but then yes! Yes! It is about a lost child! Name again? David Desouza. But before page can be –

David Fay?

Fay, are you okay?

Fay You are who you say you are?

David Fay?

Fay You are David Desouza, aren't you?

David Fay, what is this?

54

Fay You are David Desouza?

Beats.

David You're a clever girl, aren't you?

Fay What?

David You're a clever girl. Bang to rights. How did you know to ask that?

Fay Who are you?

David Am I David Desouza? Good question . . . Who am I?

I used to know. I used to know, then Katherine disappeared and now I feel like someone else.

Fay I see. Oh, I see. That not knowing who you are. I know that sort.

David You do?

Fay That sort, oh yes. Phew.

David 'Phew'? What's going on in there, Fay?

Fay Shall we sit?

You didn't tell me something important about your daughter.

I can see your dilemma. Did she walk out, was she a victim of someone, or did she commit suicide? Which of these to tell her son?

David Her previous attempt wasn't an attempt. It was a mistake. And whatever it was, it was nothing to do with drowning.

Fay You don't know that she drowned and Kevin's already explained to you that he didn't see her that night –

David Can he explain why he appears to be soaking wet? It's not raining, but he's wet. On film he leaves wet footprints, and when he attempted to harm his ex-wife there was water –

Fay She dropped those charges –

David He pushed her head under the bathwater –

Fay I spent time with him by a fucking river and he never touched me! There was no sign, no behaviour, nothing to indicate that he had it in him to be John the Baptist. People do get wrongly convicted you know; wrongly accused, wrongly labelled, wrongly convicted, wrongly condemned –

David I'm fully aware of that!

Fay You only came across Kevin after you were told what? That he was a suspect? That he'd been charged? Then of course you go with that view, no one could blame you for that. You believe what you're told by the authorities, you trust those in charge to tell you the truth, or to have checked that their facts are facts. And you've never met Kevin. I've met him, you've only seen him or written to him or read about him or been told about him. I've met him, and the evidence against him stinks!

Okay, let's just both calm down.

Do you know what your daughter was doing in the area she might have disappeared from?

David No.

Fay No idea at all?

David It's a mystery.

Fay How was her marriage?

David Stop it! How's yours?

Fay What do you mean? . . .

You mean Noah.

David I apologise. I withdraw that last remark.

Fay What do you know about him?

Look at me. What do you know about him?

David I've seen him.

Fay Seen him!

David Yes.

Fay In hospital?

David Yes.

Fay . . . You followed me there?

You are in such serious trouble! You're obsessed! You're obsessed with John the Baptist, you're obsessed with Kevin and you're becoming obsessed with me!

David Yes. Yes. Perhaps you're right.

Fay It's definitely not normal behaviour.

David For me. No . . .

To understand yourself; you'd think that would be easy. To know why you do what you do, why you react how you react. Have the attitudes you have. To be able to see that you're getting things wrong, and alter your behaviour. To use some part of you to argue with another part.

Fay I watched Noah go mad.

It was completely illogical; except there must be a logic to it.

It's all right, really. Really, it's okay. I'm over it. I'm really – you know, he left me, his mind left. It's okay. It's quite a while, actually. Nice bloke. That's just the way it is. Never harmed anyone else. Not made for this world.

Couldn't cope. It's a strange story. He's sort of female, really. His madness, the way he went, the tragedy of him, is how female madwomen are portrayed. You know, mad men are scary, unless they're old, with Alzheimer's. Men who go mad are feared. Women, though, the ones in, say, like the one in *Jane Eyre*, his first wife in the attic, and women who go mad in French films, they're sort of tragic/romantic, which is what he's like, really.

But he couldn't stand aside from it. He was in it. We're in ourselves, aren't we? I was at a low ebb when I met him. Then; wow, wow. Deep, deep, fall. Only him in the world. Him, him. We were apart only one night. Talked all that night on the phone.

I don't think Kevin is John the Baptist, because I knew him when he was young, and I know him now, and I've never felt that he could raise the necessary violence, that he can be as violent as John the Baptist.

And if it wasn't for the testimony of Michael Penn, Kevin wouldn't have been convicted.

David I've met Michael Penn.

Beats.

Fay Kevin and his legal team would very much like to know where he is.

David I don't have an address for him, or anything. It was all very cloak and dagger.

But he looked me in the eye and reiterated his statement. And Michael Penn has cast-iron alibis for two of the murders. And men who murder their own wives – or try to – don't usually murder strange women too –

Fay An argument in favour of Kevin –

David He denied he tried to harm his ex-wife – he can't have it both ways.

Fay His ex-wife, not his wife.

David Hardly a stranger, though. Obviously, Michael Penn was given a little time off for testifying against Kevin, but it wasn't excessive. His sentence was only three years in the first place.

Fay But you believe him.

David I've looked him in the eye.

Fay One of Michael Penn's alibis has fallen apart. The case against Kevin has become even more flimsy and unsafe. It's frightening that he's been convicted on so little evidence. If you believe in justice for yourself you should believe in justice for everyone.

  Beats.

David I've been to Slindon. Since Kevin wasn't charged with Katherine. Before I met you.

I tried to raise Kevin with a man I got into conversation with. I said I was passing through, that I seemed to know the name Slindon from somewhere, was it famous for anything? He said it wasn't.

I did wonder about saying who I was to several other people I met. Hard to describe who I am, though. A man who's fixed on a belief.

It's a small place, isn't it?

Fay Very.

David Here. I'll write it down for you. The police officer who set me up with Michael Penn. He had some way of contacting him. Penn called me. Number withheld and all that. I had to pay him to meet me. He's unpleasant in many respects. You know why he says Kevin confessed to him? Because he'd been telling Kevin about killing his wife. Picture the scene in that cell that night, if you can bear it.

59

You must promise me that you'll not try to meet Michael Penn yourself – you'll not try to look him in the eye. Promise me.

Fay In case he murders strange women?

I promise.

David gives number.

What does he look like?

David Superficially, a little like me with regard to his ———— and his ———— (*details as per the actor playing David*) and his accent, actually. We're from the same part of the world, geographically. That makes you smile; why?

Fay Because Kevin told the truth about something.

David The Thames is over two hundred miles long. A body's washed ashore every week. Even when you know a body's in there, if it's in the London stretch, the width, the current, make searching for it nigh impossible. A body goes in here, comes up there, miles upstream, miles down. It goes in now, it comes up, whenever. There's many variables. My life used to be normal. I used to be normal. Now I know these things. I've been to a psychic. Useless. Criminal. Couldn't really see a damn thing. I tried offering a reward for information. People tried it on; told me lies to try and get the money. I challenged one. 'I didn't mean any harm.' You're a liar, I said. You didn't *mean* any harm, but you knew there would *be* harm, that you were *causing* harm. What you *mean* when you say you didn't *mean* any harm was that you hoped that you'd get away with it, that you wouldn't be caught – *but I've caught you*!

And the water is cruel. After a short while the skin looks burned.

They call you up to say another female cadaver has risen.

You go down there. They're very kind. You can't identify her.

What if I am wrong about everything? What if my daughter's marriage was terrible – what if she just left again? She'd left before. What if my son-in-law's covering that up? What if she was a terrible wife, terrible mother? What if Katherine was really depressed again? The idea that I created a daughter who –

He's going.

Fay Don't be broken; please don't be broken.

David Oh, I'm not. Not yet.

Exit David.

TWENTY-TWO: GAOL

Fay and Kevin are opposite sides of the table. Emile monitors them.

Fay He's definitely David Desouza and he's given me the name and number of a police officer who can get hold of Michael Penn. I had it written down for you but they confiscated it when they searched me.

Kevin Tell it me now.

Fay I can't remember it.

Kevin Try.

Fay I didn't memorise it.

Kevin This is important, Fay.

Fay That's why I passed it to Mr Bullock as well.

Kevin It's the name and number of the copper who told David Desouza how to get hold of Michael Penn?

Fay Yes.

Kevin Not Michael Penn's number?

Fay No. Michael Penn phoned David Desouza.

Kevin So David Desouza has his number?

Fay He says it was withheld.

Beats.

Kevin Well, it's something.

Fay If I'd've known they were going to confiscate it I'd've memorised it. Mr Bullock'll get it in the post, and it's at reception here. Okay?

Kevin Okay. It could help. Mr Bullock can argue that a police officer knows where Michael Penn is, so they have to disclose it. And if they don't, then we can accuse them of something.

Thank David Desouza for me, next time you see him.

Thank him for me, you promise? And thank yourself. Give yourself a treat. Thank you, Fay. Thank you. Will David Desouza accept my thanks?

Fay It might be difficult for him.

Kevin Yeah . . . He thinks I had sex with his daughter.

Fay Does he?

Kevin He thinks I'm John the Baptist.

Fay John the Baptist didn't have sex with those women! That wasn't sex!

Kevin All right, all right. I said the wrong thing, I'm sorry. I'm sorry. Look, I'm sorry.

Are we having our first proper row? I'm really sorry. If I could nip to the florist's I would. Fay?

Fay? Is this what you were like with your ex-husband? Fay the fiery. You're a good woman, you know, visiting him. You visit him; you visit me. Who else visits him?

Who's he with now?

Fay?

Fay We haven't been together, at home, for nearly three years.

Kevin What are you saying, Fay?

Fay To all intents and purposes I'm not married, because my husband's gone away. The man I married no longer exists. He's disappeared.

Kevin You told me a little porky, didn't you, Fay?

Fay I could divorce him. I'd decided to divorce him.

Kevin I forgive you.

It's great what you've done for me. We'll end up with Michael Penn in here, me out there. Penn penned up, me free. Let's hope that that little bit of info you got helps.

I know you know what else would make a big difference to my appeal. It's a little thing. One little thing for you, one giant thing for me.

Fay ?

Kevin Okay – a guessing game. You said it's a shame I don't have any.

Fay Any what?

Kevin . . . Okay. Pick a date.

Fay A date for what?

Kevin For us.

Fay For us?

Kevin There's five possible dates, when we were on a date.

Fay I can tell you the date we were down by the river, it was –

Kevin Not that far back. I've been wrongly convicted of five crimes, on five dates. If we were together on one or more of those dates . . .

It might seem like a confession that you'd been unfaithful to your husband, but if he was away at the time, people will understand.

What?

Fay It wouldn't be the truth.

Kevin It's a little lie, fighting the cause of a big truth. It'd be a good lie. Bad lies put me in here, a good lie could help to get me out.

Fay But they'll ask why I didn't come forward before?

Kevin Because you didn't want to upset your husband.

Fay?

Fay? Please, Fay, I'm begging you.

I know I'll be freed, but it could take years. With your help things would speed right up.

Fay, please.

> Fay, Fay,
> I asked her today
> To help me
> And what did she say?

I've been busy reading letters from other women. There's a promising one named Sandra who I'm thinking of inviting down. She's started a campaign for me.

Emile What's that item?

Kevin It's a paper handkerchief. She's crying.

Emile inspects the crumpled paper handkerchief then returns it to Fay and moves on.

Kevin Fay White, the golden girl of Slindon. How come you're having the life you're having, Fay?

Fay I don't know.

Emile nears. He sees that she's still upset.

Emile Everything all right?

Fay Yes.

Beats.

Emile moves away.

Kevin sings 'The River', distractedly. Fay's in her own thoughts.

Kevin segues into making small, quiet sounds, which at first Fay fails to pick up on. His voice has gone up in pitch. Fay's surprised out of her reverie. She watches, transfixed, horrified, as Kevin's words – in this alien voice – gradually become clear.

Kevin Oh, please,

Oh please,

Oh please.

No, don't.

Don't.

I beg you.

Beg you.

Help!

Help!

Then Kevin's back. Looking at her normally, and Fay can't decide what just happened.

Emile What just happened there?

Kevin I don't know –

Emile What just happened?

Kevin Nothing –

Emile I'm not asking you.

Fay Nothing happened.

Emile Then why were you looking like that?

Fay I don't know. I didn't mean to look like whatever I looked like.

Emile moves away.

Kevin Are you all right, Fay?

Fay Yes. Are you?

Kevin Yes.

Fay Why were your feet wet?

Kevin My feet?

Fay I didn't mean to ask that.

Kevin But you have asked.

Fay I didn't mean to.

Kevin What do you mean, 'Why were my feet wet?'

Fay When you were running away from the muggers you left wet footprints.

Kevin I ran through a puddle.

Fay But it hadn't rained for over a week.

Kevin Not all puddles are rainwater, Fay. I don't know how the puddle got there. Perhaps it was piss.

Fay I'm going to have to talk to someone.

Kevin Talk to someone?

Fay Yes.

Kevin Talk to who about what?

Fay About what just happened.

Kevin What just happened?

Fay I don't know.

Kevin Are you threatening me?

Fay No.

Kevin What are you doing, then?

Emile comes over.

Fay I'm leaving, actually. I'd like to go, now, please.

Kevin She's angry and upset because we've probably split up.

Emile Good. Congratulations.

Kevin She lied that her marriage was over, you know.

Fay No, I'm not going.

I'm really sorry that I didn't do something different that special day we had back home. If I'd said or done something different we probably wouldn't be where we are now.

Kevin Fay –

Fay But we have to deal with where we are now, not where we'd like to be. I don't know what just happened but already I can't stop thinking about it – and I don't want to leave you confused about it, and about what I meant when I said I needed to talk to someone about it. I don't honestly know if you know what happened, but that is beside the –

Kevin Fay, stop talking –

Fay If I hear that you are going ahead with your appeal I have no choice but to –

Kevin Fay –

Fay – come forward and tell what happened . . .

Kevin What happened? Tell me what happened?

If you can't tell me, then what can I do? How can I defend myself when I don't know what I'm accused of?

Fay If you appeal I shall have to try and find words to convey –

Kevin I'm appealing to you, I'm appealing to you now to tell me what happened – this thing that you'll try to tell someone.

Fay I will have to be at your appeal to tell my story –

Kevin Your story – whaddya mean, 'your story'?

Fay I'll have to. I'll just have to, Kevin.

She's going. Kevin rises.

Kevin (*in his own voice*) No, don't.

Don't.

I beg you.

Emile restrains him.

Help! Help!

I beg you. Beg you.

Fay! Please!

Emile shoves Kevin out of the room, into the prison.

Emile (*to Fay*) You okay?

TWENTY-THREE: PARK

David Has something happened?

Fay You leap from certainty to certainty, digging your nails in, trying to hang on like some stupid animal –

David You've found something out, haven't you?

Fay Watching me must be like watching some stupid, trembling animal – some stupid fluttering thing that you don't have to take very seriously –

David Is it something about Katherine?

Fay – an animal after a bush fire or a flood, when everything's destroyed or swept away –

David Tell me what's happened, what's changed, why you're upset like this.

Fay – in a permanent stampede . . .

David Did he say anything about Katherine? Just tell me!

David grabs Fay.

Fay doesn't react to his violence.

David regrets grabbing her and lets her go.

Fay Show me Katherine's photo again. (*Takes it. After a while she greets it.*) . . . Hello, Katherine Desouza.

David But you now believe that Kevin is John the Baptist, don't you?

Fay (*returns the photo of Katherine*) I don't have the answer to her disappearance.

I love Noah. I love my husband. I wish he'd return. He's got himself lost somewhere. He went out too far and he can't find his way home. He'll come home. I'm his beacon. He'll come home. And Katherine, she'll come home. I'm going to go and tell Noah that he has to come back so that he can meet you. I'm going to tell him come back and meet this man.

TWENTY-FOUR: DAVID

David Time passes.

Once a week, Fay and I meet and engross each other. And I'm happy to report that we're engaged in a great friendship. Completely unexpected, unanticipated. To be cherished. We meet in the park if fine, the bookshop – which to all intents and purposes is our club – if not. And we argue about books and people and this and that and that and –

It is comforting. It is a considerable consolation, to spend time together, knowing that the other is possibly thinking of similar things.

And sometimes you think, how could a man do what the devil known as John the Baptist did – how can a man find that that sort of behaviour gives him an erection? And you try not to think of the details, but sometimes they overwhelm you. If you have a mind for questions, unpleasant questions will arise. And you try not to think about how the last face they saw was John the Baptist's – if they saw it, and the last words they heard – if he uttered any – were from his mouth. And you also think of Katherine alive somewhere, perhaps; and of Noah, still not returned, still not with us. Both still not found.

I observe that my son-in-law is very carefully, very gently planning life without my daughter. You hope for him. And Freddy, my grandson, hasn't asked me about his mother for a while. He's begun to collect anything to do with angels; pictures, small plastic figures . . . I thought that I saw her again today.

We live with uncertainty.

End.